M. V. B. Phillips

# Life and Death in Andersonville

Or, What I Saw and Experienced During Seven Months in Rebel Prisons

M. V. B. Phillips

**Life and Death in Andersonville**
*Or, What I Saw and Experienced During Seven Months in Rebel Prisons*

ISBN/EAN: 9783744792288

Printed in Europe, USA, Canada, Australia, Japan

Cover: Foto ©ninafisch / pixelio.de

More available books at **www.hansebooks.com**

# Life and Death in Andersonville;

OR,

## What I Saw and Experienced During Seven Months in Rebel Prisons.

———◦❯❮◦———

By Rev. M. V. B. PHILLIPS,

OF KANSAS.

———◦❯❮◦———

T. B. ARNOLD, 104-6 FRANKLIN STREET, CHICAGO,
1887.

# TABLE OF CONTENTS.

# PREFACE.

EVERY blessing that we enjoy, either great or small, as a general thing, has cost somebody something; either mental labor, physical exertion, money, suffering, or death.

To procure us a free pardon and exemption from eternal death cost the Son of God terrible suffering and death.

Look at the first colonies of this country. Their inhabitants were reduced in numbers, and subjected to extreme want, and many perished.

Look, again, at the suffering undergone by the Revolutionary soldiers while they struggled for freedom from the oppression of a monarchical government, after the colonies had been established.

Once more I ask all who can comprehend the thousandth part of the suffering caused by the War of the Rebellion, to see what it cost in broken families, broken hearts, privations, distress and death of the fathers, mothers, wives and soldiers of that conflict. These heroes left their comfortable homes and stepped in front of the deadly cannon and musketry, belching destruction and death at every volley, on a thousand battlefields, to save for you this country, that was about to be torn into fragments and destroyed by ambitious and selfish men.

It would seem as if any loyal citizen, having a capacity to comprehend what the present prosperity and liberties that we now enjoy cost the soldiers of the Rebellion, and especially the fraction of them described in this little book, and yet feels that he is under little or no obligation to them, or would object to perpetuating their memory, is an ingrate who can hardly be accounted for or excused by all loyal and grateful people.

If it should be thought by a few that such a book has a tendency to stir up the remaining rebel spirit in the South, I am led to exclaim, "Oh, what an idea!" All who have been truly sorry for their treason, and for the great amount of suffering that they caused, will not be stirred up by this recital. Those who have not repented of the great wrong they have done ought to be reminded of this sin until they repent.

If the logic holds good that it is wrong to remind sinners of their crimes in the South, either national or individual, then let the ministers at the North cease to ferment strife by telling the people, in their discourses, of their past sins.

Further, if it is wrong for the soldier of the Rebellion to tell his experience in suffering because some in the South might not like it, then wipe out of history the deeds and sufferings of the soldiers of the Revolution, and let nothing further of this be written, for there are English people in Great Britain and this country who might be offended by the record.

In sending out this little book, it is hoped that it may fall into the hands of some of the rising generation who have come upon the stage of action since the war. It is small in size and cost, and will enable all who have heard of Andersonville, but have never read of the terrible sufferings of those who were imprisoned there, or in the military prisons of the South, to understand what our soldiers there endured.

The writer is a sufferer. He has lost his voice and hearing; has throat and lung disease, and a terrible cough; a constant roaring in the head, night and day, and a general debility that incapacitates him for any kind of business or exertion. These afflictions, all physicians say, arise from catarrh. The disease was contracted, in its mildest form, in the service, and has gradually increased until it has become what it is at present. He receives no pension from the government, although he has applied for one.

If this little book continues to receive favorable notice in the future, as it has since I gave notice of my intention to publish it, we hope, by its sale, to be somewhat benefited in our limited resources.

THE AUTHOR.

the fall and winter of 1861–'62. Early in the spring of 1862 we moved under General Pope against New Madrid, Mo. This was our first engagement. Here we heard the first "whiz" of the enemy's bullets; here we heard the first screech of the terrible shell, as it burst in our midst. We captured the place after a short siege, together with Island Number Ten and all the Confederate men and implements of war that were stationed there.

This was about the time of the memorable battle of Shiloh, on the Tennessee River, and we were hurried into boats and transported up the rivers until we arrived, a few days after that terrible fight, at Hamburg Landing, eight miles above Pittsburg Landing, on the Tennessee, and re-enforced the shattered forces there.

On May 9, 1862, we had our second engagement, at Farming, Miss., near Corinth. In this fight my brother, David T. Phillips, was killed. He belonged to the same company as myself, and at that time we were both on the skirmish-line, in advance of the whole army. He was only a short distance from me when he fell. I was with him in a few minutes, and found that he had been shot in the shoulder, the ball coming out near the spine, and he was bleeding frightfully. (I gathered up some cotton that was handy, and, pressing it upon the wounds, stopped the flow of blood. I then went for help) and we succeeded in carrying him off the field in time to save ourselves from capture. He lived a few hours afterward, and when he died he was buried in a pine box, shrouded in the clothes in which he had been killed. His bones still lie down in Mississippi, with no stone or board to mark his grave.

The next engagement in which I participated was of a more general character, on May 28, near Corinth, Mississippi.

Soon after this conflict, the rebels evacuated Corinth, and we encamped at Danville, Miss., until in September. In that month we marched twenty-eight miles, to Iuka, where we encountered General Price and had a severe fight. We then fell back to Corinth, and had another terrible conflict, which lasted two days. This battle was fought October 2 and 3, 1862.

The next engagement in which I had a part was that of Missionary Ridge, in Tennessee, soon after the unfortunate defeat of General Rosecrans. This was a hard fight, and in one charge we lost a little more than one-fourth of our regiment.

We gained the victory here, and immediately afterward marched to Knoxville, Tenn., a distance of one hundred miles, to relieve General Burnside, who was there besieged by Longstreet. During this march we "lived off the country." Previous to this advance we had marched from Memphis to Chattanooga.

During these last marches and fights our regiment belonged to the Fifteenth Army Corps—General Sherman's, but at this time commanded by General John A. Logan—and with which corps we remained throughout the war.

In our brigade we were in company with the "Eagle Regiment," the Eighth Wisconsin, and went through the rebellion in sight of the famous eagle "Old Abe," for whom the regiment was named. No doubt the reader remembers having seen his photograph in many an album.

### A HALT.

AFTER these marches and engagements we encamped for the winter at Scottsborough, Ala., where the largest number of the men in our regiment became veterans. I did not re-enlist.

### THE MARCH TO THE SEA.

THE following summer our brigade started with General Sherman on his remarkable march to the sea. A few days after leaving camp we had a hard fight at Resaca, and on our march there was fighting and skirmishing almost every day, until we reached Atlanta, Ga. Here the rebels made a determined stand, and brought on a general engagement, which began on July 22, 1864. This event brings me to the date of

### MY CAPTURE.

I HAD been on the skirmish-line, in advance of the the army, for over twenty-four hours. The main force had reached a point within a short distance of the suburbs of Atlanta, and this movement led the rebels to make a charge upon us in force, and we fell back to our main line of battle, which was in readiness to receive them.

Our artillery commenced throwing shell, grape and canister-shot into the woods in the direction of the charging columns of rebels, who were then at some distance off. Before I could reach our lines I accidentally came before one of our batteries, and discovered that I was between two fires—the charging rebels in the rear, and our own line of battle in front.

It was frequently the case, during the war, that the skirmishers did not get back to our main army, in the event of a charge, before it became necessary for our lines to open fire on the enemy. As soon as I comprehended the situation I made double-quick time in front of our battery, keeping as well between the ranges of the different guns as I could, and thus came safely within our lines. But I did not know where to find my company or the regiment, it having been moved during my absence; neither had I time to hunt for it, for a momentous engagement was at hand. Coming upon the Ninetieth Illinois Regiment of Infantry, I joined it and remained with it until it was driven back to our second line of intrenchments, when I retreated with it. A lull in the battle ensued, and comparative silence prevailed after the terrible roar of artillery and musketry, in which thousands of guns had simultaneously participated.

During this short silence I saw John A. Logan dash by, and learned that he was to take General McPherson's position, and command the left wing of Sherman's army, General McPherson having been killed but a few minutes before. The left wing, at this time, comprised at least three corps, including ours (the Fifteenth), which General Logan had, up to this period, commanded. I also learned that the reserves were coming up, and that within a few minutes our forces were going to charge the enemy and recapture what we had lost in the recent attack.

From an officer, who thought he knew, I learned that my company and regiment were still holding their position on the left, in the direction of some firing that we then heard. I decided that if they were there, I could, by running some risk, get to them. With this purpose in view I started along, with my gun at a trail, and moving in double-quick time in the specified direction, pushing through the brush and timber along my route. I had not proceeded more than half a mile when I heard the word "HALT!" shouted from a thick cluster of small trees, about two rods from me. I looked up in surprise, and found myself confronted by five rebels, each having his gun at his shoulder, cocked, and aimed directly at me.

In the excitement of the moment, I did a very foolish thing, that came very near costing me my life then and there. As soon as I saw that it was rebels who had "halted" me, without a thought of the consequences, I instantly cocked my gun and leveled it at them.

They were not expecting this, but supposed, of course, that I would, upon seeing my situation, immediately surrender. They had been watching me for some time as I approached. They had no desire to kill me, but intended to secure me as a prisoner. But when they saw my reckless daring, each of the five brought his gun to his face and pointed it at my heart, at about the distance of two rods from me. Under these desperate circumstances, in less time than it took to make my first thoughtless threat, I reversed matters by dropping the muzzle of my gun on the ground, and at the same time raising my cap from my head with my left hand. It was all done with so much rapidity that before they could fire at me they saw that I had surrendered.

Up to this moment I had not spoken; but when I heard one of them say, in a loud tone, to the others, "Don't shoot—he surrenders," I added, "Of course I surrender;" still standing and holding up the breech of my weapon with my right hand, with its muzzle on the ground, and lifting my cap over my head with the left.

Then came the order to "Come up!" each rebel continuing to keep his gun to his eye, aimed at my breast, and his finger on the trigger.

I knew that my life for the next few moments depended upon my discretion and great caution in my movements. The least indication, on my part, either of contumacy or of an intention to escape, would have been sufficient cause for them to pierce my body with five minie bullets.

At their command to "Come up!" I let go of the breech of my gun, letting it fall to the ground.

Then came the order, "Bring your gun!"

I said, "All right;" but added that they had better permit me to let down its hammer (for it was still cocked); and they also replied, "All right."

With this permission I cautiously lifted the gun by its breech, leaving the muzzle on the ground, and let down the hammer. Then I took up the weapon, and carried it at a trail, and facing their five deadly muskets, until I halted before them. .

# CHAPTER II.

AFTER I reached them, and they had taken possession of my gun, they were quite friendly, asking me many questions. I had conversed with them only a few moments before I told them that if they were going to hold me as a prisoner, I wished they would take me back and place me in the rear of their army, adding that "they would have fun" here directly.

I knew our forces were about ready and would shell them in a short time, then charge upon them and recapture the ground which we had lost a few hours before.

Upon receiving this information they seemed to be somewhat alarmed, and as anxious to get to the rear as I was. They started immediately with me, but we had not gone more than one hundred yards before we crossed their main line of battle, lying on the opposite side of the trenches which they had captured from us. I picked up a roll of blankets that our soldiers had left during the rebel charge, and passed on, with one guard, to the rear. We had gone but a few rods when our artillery opened fire on them with grape and canister. I do not believe that during the war I was under a more galling fire, or in more danger, than I was in the few minutes that I was moving on the "double-quick" to get out of range of our guns. My first guard had his shoulder crushed by a missile. I was then taken in charge by another, and we made good time until we got from under fire.

One mean rebel took the rubber blanket from the roll that I had picked up. I thought, for awhile, that I was the only prisoner captured, as I saw no others till I had nearly reached Atlanta. But before 9 o'clock in the evening they had 1,800 of us gathered in a bunch in that city.

We were marched out, that night, to Jonesborough, nine miles south of Atlanta, at which place we probably arrived at midnight or later. There we were corralled in as small a compass as possible and permitted to lie down on the ground and sleep till morning. About sunrise I awoke and arose to see if there were any prisoners whom I knew, and, to my surprise, I saw my own captain—J. S. Lothrop—coming towards me. He had discovered me first. It was the first intimation that he had of my being a prisoner. We both tried to be cheerful, and laughed, the captain remarking that we were "in rather a bad box." From him I learned that two more of my company had also been captured and were then in the corral—F. Demings and C. Babcock.

The commissioned officers were soon separated from us and sent, I believe, to Macon, Ga. The rest of us marched one day, after leaving Jonesborough, and were then loaded into railroad box-cars and sent directly through to

## ANDERSONVILLE.

WE arrived at Andersonville July 28. There the train stopped between two lines of rebel infantry, standing shoulder to shoulder, with fixed bayonets, in the position for making a charge. We were now ordered to leave the cars, and marched between two similar lines of soldiers until within a few yards of the stockade, or prison, which was only a few rods from the station.

I am unable to describe my feelings as I came in sight of the prison. It was so situated, and so near, that I could look inside of it. There I saw thousands of living human skeletons moving about, half-naked, in the hot, broiling sun, on an open space, with not a bush of any description. I had seen enough of misery in my first view of the prison, and that at a distance, to surpass all the newspaper reports I had ever read relating to these Southern pens of death, or that my imagination had ever pictured of the misery they contained; but the worst is yet to be told.

On the way hither we had been told by the guards that we were going into good barracks, with plenty of everything to make us reasonably comfortable.

Coming near the gate of the stockade, we were formed in line to be searched. All money of the denomination of one dollar and upward that our captors found was taken from us, together with our watches, knives, case-knives, etc. Greenbacks, among the rebels, were about as valuable as at the North, and if a prisoner succeeded in getting into the prison with his money he could use it, secretly, to good advantage. The rebels dared not handle it in trade openly, but many were gathering as much of it as they could, slyly, for future use, by giving a $10 Confederate note for a $1 greenback. The men who visited the prison every day, to call the roll of the different companies, were aware that many of us had brought in money by secreting it in our clothing. The rebels were anxious to trade off their money, on the sly, for ours, and for this reason would not take undue advantage of the Union men, but extended friendly inducements for them to part with it. By this traffic, too, the prisoners reaped considerable advantage; for with the Confederate currency they could purchase goods of the rebel sutler, who was commissioned to sell them to those in the prison, but who did not dare to receive greenbacks openly.

During the search I first saw Captain Wirz, the keeper of the stockade, who was hanged at Washington, when the war ended, for his barbarity toward the prisoners. I must say that he was the most inhuman and abusive man that I ever met; and before the search was finished he flew into a rage and came very near shooting me. The circumstances were these: I was gazing so intently into the prison that I did not hear the command given to "dress up," and was aroused by seeing the captain standing before me with a revolver pointed toward my person. I stepped into line as soon as I could, for I perceived wherein the trouble arose, and felt that I had once more narrowly escaped death.

When the search was concluded, the prison gate was thrown open, and we were marched within the walls of Andersonville.

The majority of them had something to sell, and all were holding up the articles with their skeleton and sun-burnt arms, and each was crying at the top of his voice, in order to be heard above the others: "Who will give me ten cents for this spoon?" "Who will give me twenty-five cents for this knife?" etc. Spoons, knives and forks, canteens, shirts, blankets and similar wares were on the market. The scene, the noise, and the general condition of the prison and its inmates, so bewildered me at first that for a few moments everything turned dark, and I wondered where I was—whether it was a dream, or whether I was not in some place where demons reveled, or whether this was indeed the dreadful Andersonville Prison.

### SEEKING REST.

But I soon rallied, and, taking in the reality of the situation, began to look for a "local habitation." The ground was very nearly all occupied. Only a few vacant places remained, and those living near them pretended to have a claim upon them. Demings and Babcock, my company comrades, were with me, and every time we attempted to settle on a lot, those near it would exclaim: "You can't stop there—get out o' that!" etc. We tried several localities, and the result was everywhere the same. Finally Demings said that if we got a place, we would have to take and hold it by force. The next vacant spot we found, Demings cried out, "Here 's a good place!"

"Get out o' that!—you can't stop there!" came from many throats in all quarters.

We laid down our things, and told our companions

that if they were able to put us off we would go, but if
not we would remain. This ended the controversy.
They saw that we were fresh prisoners and were in too
good condition for them to attack.

### DESCRIPTION OF THE PRISON.

THE stockade was fashioned from pine timber and
inclosed about twenty-three acres of land. The walls
were composed of pine logs set on end, one against the
other, and about twelve or fifteen feet high. Every
few yards, on the outside, at the top of the stockade,
was a sentinel-stand, and a guard on each, his head and
shoulders visible above the wall, and armed with a loaded
gun, watching to see that none violated the prison rules.
If any did they were shot. The *dead-line* was a pole
fastened to a post on the inside of the prison. It was
about twenty feet upon the stockade—placed at that
distance to keep the prisoners from tunneling out at
night. It was instant death, without warning, to cross it.

### SHELTER.

THE prisoners were not furnished, by the rebels, with
barracks, sheds, tents, or any description of shelter, or
materials to make it. It mattered not how destitute they
were on entering; they were turned in and left to do the
best they could with whatever they had. Many, of
course, who had been captured in warm weather, were
without blankets; many more were robbed, as I had
been, or in other ways were deprived of necessary
covering. Those who had blankets would manage to
obtain three slender poles—two for end-supports, each
four or five feet long, and a ridge-pole, and, by stretch-

ing a blanket over this frame, could secure shelter from the heat of the sun, and partially so from rain. This was the kind mostly constructed by a majority of the 33,000 prisoners while I was an inmate of the stockade, during the months of August, September and October.

A number who had been brought into the stockade soon after it was finished were more fortunate, as they had the privilege of using some of the tops and limbs of the trees from which the prison was built. With these they erected better quarters, by leaning sticks up against a ridge-pole and covering them with brush, leaves and dirt.

Very many unfortunate ones, who had been imprisoned without either blankets or money, were destitute of any shelter or covering, unless they found some intimate friend or comrade, who had shelter, to share it with them. Strangers would seldom be so obliging. It was a matter of life and death with all, and they acted on the principles adopted by capitalists when going into business—they mated with those who had as much material for comfort as themselves.

Many poor fellows lay exposed to the weather for weeks, unable to obtain shelter. This, too, was in the warm season; and yet I have heard them running, during the latter part of the night, to warm their chilled bodies and limbs. Of course they did not long survive the cooler weather of the autumnal months. Of these, and their sad fate, I may have occasion to speak more fully in a future chapter.

### STREETS.

OUR quarters were not constructed, as to their location, with much regularity. There were immethodical streets, about a rod wide, running one way. The quarters were generally "parked" one against another along these pathways. I think this inhabitable part of the prison averaged five persons to every square rod of surface; some places were more densely populated than others.

# CHAPTER IV.

Food, Cooked and Uncooked—Quantity and Quality—Issuing Rations—Insect Annoyances, etc.

NEXT in order I will sketch the character of our food, previous to describing the sickness, misery and death in our prison; and the one will aid the reader in understanding why there was so much of the other among us.

During my stay in Andersonville one-half of the prisoners were provided with their rations cooked, while the other half devoured theirs raw. The cooked food consisted of a piece of corn-bread, made out of unbolted meal, about four inches long, two and a half inches wide, and two inches thick; a pint of boiled brown peas, and a piece of thin bacon, two inches square. This was one day's ration. I feel sure that I have stated the quantity sufficiently large.

## QUALITY OF RATIONS.

THE provisions were brought to us in two-horse wagons. The peas were boiled almost to a mush. They were issued to the commissaries of companies, the same as in the army, and subdivided and distributed to each person. For want of utensils in which to draw the company rations, they were collected in rubber blankets owned by some of the company. Numerous individuals had not even a cup in which to draw their quantum of peas, and so used their caps, the corners of their blouses, or the pockets of their pantaloons, which they had torn from the garments for this purpose.

The peas looked as though they had been trampled out, or threshed out with flails, on the ground, and winnowed in the wind. They were full of dirt, pea-pods, stones, etc. But the most incredible story about these peas is yet to be told. It was at a season of the year when there seemed to be a pea-bug in every pea, such as nearly every person at the North has seen in our domestic peas; and these bugs were visible, after we had drawn them, all through the ration, look-ing like black pepper.

The first peas I drew after becoming a prisoner I thought I could not eat, unless I could remove the bugs by putting them into a cup, pouring boiling water upon them and stirring up the mess, in hopes the insects would rise to the surface. I succeeded in dis-lodging a few of them in this manner, but found, also, that I had washed away much of the substance of the peas. By the time I had drawn the next day's ration I was hungry enough to eat them, as the older prison-ers did—bugs and all.

The bacon issued to us was boiled with the peas, and often it was honey-combed with worms. My first ration was in this condition. The fleshy side was covered with a white slime that I believed was caused by the boiled worms coming to the surface of the meat. I asked a prisoner for a knife, and cut off a thin flake that contained the slime (or worm-juice, as I thought), and was in the act of throwing it away, when the owner of the knife said, "Give it to me." I did so, and he ate it, remarking that I would "get over that in a few days."

I relate these incidents to show what hungry and helpless men will eat and be glad of the opportunity.

Many, no doubt, will read this and wonder that human stomachs can become accustomed to receive such filthy food. I will say to such, that starvation will drive away all delicacy of taste and digestion. It is simply the want of experience that leads one to doubt the truth of such horrible revelations. One may have been hungry; one may have been *very* hungry, and not have been driven to such extremities, but it was because food, and good food, was expected soon.

The reason why many cannot readily believe the numerous instances of human endurance in the great sufferings of prisoners, related by other writers, is because they have never seen human nature put to the rack and brought to the direst condition. They do not know what humanity can endure. They may have seen, as I have in prison, one or two individuals give way to a small, unaccustomed pressure; but I have known others to endure to a degree that I could scarcely credit, unless I had myself witnessed it.

One-half of the prisoners (numbering about 15,000) received about the same quantity and quality of food as the others, but it was in the raw material. It is necessary for me to state, before closing this chapter, that, during my stay in the prison, there was no change in our articles of diet, or the manner of their distribution, in any important particular. The thousands of sick men, of all grades, there confined, received the same sort of provisions, with no variation, as the other prisoners. I cannot speak for the invalids in the hospital; they were outside of the stockade.

# CHAPTER V.

IT will be necessary, in this chapter, to give a description of the cooking utensils, seeing that so many
were obliged to prepare their own rations. In their
necessities the rebels failed to furnish anything, and
whatever a man took into the prison with him generally constituted his outfit during his stay.

There were prisoners in Andersonville from every
prison in the South. They had been massed there to
prevent their capture by our army. Many of them
had, when captured, more conveniences for cooking
than others. All were not robbed alike, so that many
brought with them better outfits than their fellow-
prisoners. A large number owned, each, a fry-pan, a
tin pail or coffee pot, a tin cup, a spoon, and a knife
and fork. These were considered well-prepared. Others, again, had one or two of these utensils, while many
possessed nothing of this kind. This last class were
very unfortunate. Some who had tin pails, cups, or
fruit-cans, soon found them leaking and spoiled in the
using. For this last reason it was difficult to borrow
such articles, unless one had a friend. If you loaned
your cooking kettles, and had them spoiled by the bor-
rower, you had to do without.

Those who had fry-pans could bake their meal
ration. Many baked theirs on tin pans by propping
them up before the fire. Some, who had no other

means, baked theirs as well as they could on smooth chips, in the same manner. The majority, however, made their meal into thin mush, or gruel.

### WOOD.

THIS was a very scarce article after the prison had been occupied a few weeks. At first the inmates used the tops and brush that had been left inside the stockade when it was finished; but at the time of my entrance this resource had vanished; even the stumps had been dug out, and I saw some prisoners digging deeply into the ground in search of roots as large as one's arm, or less. If I remember rightly, the rebels did not furnish much wood to those who received raw rations. On this point my memory fails me. While in Andersonville I drew my rations cooked. If wood was furnished to any, it was in very small quantities, you may know; otherwise the prisoners would not have exerted themselves as they did to obtain stumps and roots.

With such a scarcity of wood and such inferior cooking utensils, it was impossible to more than half-cook the meal and peas, and a majority of the prisoners ate their food in this condition. Under these circumstances, and in this particular, the recipients of cooked rations were better off than those who drew the raw material.

### WATER.

THERE was a small creek running through the inclosure, the ground in which rose gradually on each side of the stream. The effect was to lower the level of the stockade where it crossed the creek and the bottom-land, until we could see out beyond the walls of the prison in two directions, when we stood upon the higher ground, and those outside of the stockade could, for the same reason, look in upon us. I mention this to explain why, before I was admitted at the gate, I had looked over the wall and seen the inmates. Many might wonder how this had been done, as the wall was fifteen or eighteen feet high; and I hope this explanation will serve to elucidate other apparent difficulties in this narrative. Remember that it is impossible, in a pamphlet like this, to enter into minute details, but everything related here can be as satisfactorily explained as this one incident.

If I remember correctly, the creek was about four or five feet wide. The lower part was arranged for the private resort of the prisoners, but was not enclosed. The upper end of the stream was set apart for drinking and cooking purposes, and generally used until the "great spring" came bubbling up through the ground. This (I think) was in September, and was looked upon by many as a providential circumstance. The rebels had been digging and making some repairs inside the stockade, near the creek. There came a heavy rain—I think it was that same night—and washed the spot where they had dug to a depth that uncovered the spring; and the next morning there was a stream of cool, clear water flowing from it, sufficient, when properly arranged, to supply the prison. Besides this, there were a few other wells, which had been dug by private companies, at a considerable expense of time and with great danger. The implements used were, generally, tin plates or halves of canteens, instead of spades. The dirt and sand were loosened with knives, railroad spikes,

the slops from the cook-house, where rations for 15,000 men were prepared, went into it. Then, too, the water was warm during the hot months.

To sum up: The prisoners bathed and washed inside,—and they could not help it, for the lower end was unfit for that purpose; the cook-house above, and a whole camp of soldiers using it as I have before stated, and the natural heat of the location; consider these things, and you will form some idea of the water that we had to use for months.

### INHUMANITY.

WHY the rebels encamped above, instead of below; why they did not furnish the prisoners proper implements for digging wells, and why they did not provide for them clothing, blankets and shelter (especially for those who were extremely destitute), and other conveniences, as they might have done with little expense, is a mystery for rebel sympathizers to solve. It was stated, however, that Captain Wirz said that whatever prisoners he could not kill by gradual starvation and privation he would render unfit for any service in the Union army when released. It was almost universally believed by the prisoners that the plan was designed by the rebel government, and not by Captain Wirz alone, to gradually starve us to death and destroy as many as possible by the course he was pursuing. It certainly looked so; every indication of it was manifested in the systematic neglect and inhumanity that existed.

If it be asked why they did not starve us to death at once, if this was their plan, I answer that the fear of retaliation in the North, and the interference of foreign nations, prevented such wholesale barbarity.

Many friends of the Union, and even the government, attributed all the suffering at Andersonville to Captain Wirz, and put him alone to death, while he, as a subordinate officer, with a captain's commission, worked under the immediate orders, in controlling the prison and its inmates, of a Confederate General, whose headquarters were in sight of us everyday, and who had command of all. He knew what Captain Wirz was doing. Why was *he* not hanged? Wirz was a tyrant, but not more so than those from whom he received his orders. I always did look upon it as cowardly in our government to hang him alone. But the people were thirsting for blood; somebody must die; so they hanged an old inferior captain of the rebel army, and let the rest go. The government has permitted them to resume their old seats in Congress, and they are there to-day, working with the President, killing pension and relief bills for the benefit of these thousands of prisoners and other disabled Union soldiers.

# CHAPTER VI.

Sickness—Lice—Maggots—Flies—Other Filth.

IN this chapter I shall attempt to describe the sickness and some other sources of the misery that I saw and suffered daily; but I shall not be able to depict a thousandth part of it. I will merely give a few particular instances as examples of the many that I could present, and which have already been described by other writers.

## HOSPITAL PATIENTS.

I CANNOT say much for the hospital. It was outside of the prison, and I never entered it; and my object, in this pamphlet, is to describe only what I saw and experienced. It is proper to add, however, that I was informed, by those who knew, that the hospital was no building, or inclosure, but a shed with brush and leaves thrown over it for a covering.

Inside the prison several thousand men were sick, and in different stages of disease. They were not removed to the hospital—the rebels said—because there was no room for them in the institution; nor did any receive medical treatment in the prison.

As fast as prisoners died in the hospital enough sick ones were taken there from the prison to fill the vacant places. The method of removal was this: In the morning the prisoners would lay their sick comrade in a blanket, and four of them, one at each corner, would carry him to the prison gate. There they laid him on the ground and waited for the doctor's arrival. When he came he would select as many of the waiting invalids as there was room for in the hospital. These were carried away, and the rejected ones were taken back to their respective quarters. Many were carried to the gate and returned, for several days in succession, and perhaps never succeeded in getting to the hospital before death released them. These died in the prison without medical care. Often they departed while lying in the sun at the gate, waiting for the doctor, who generally took his own time for coming. Others, again, would frequently be exposed to the sunshine an hour or two before they learned what disposition he would make of them.

The regulations required a prisoner to be so sick that it would be necessary to carry him out in a blanket before he was eligible to go into the hospital.

There were but few messes of four or five prisoners who had been in the prison a few months, that did not have one or more such cases as I have been describing; caused by chronic disease of the bowels, induced, it was supposed, by the constant use of one kind of inferior feed, yet traceable to other causes. Many others, for the same reason, were nearly destroyed by scurvy.

In all parts of the prison were many very sick and weak ones who were unable to go to the private quarters at the creek, nor could they walk or crawl further than the sides or ends of their own quarters. In addition, these places were made receptacles for the accumulation of other filth, such as the slops of the cooking, etc. The effect of this, in many parts of the camp, was to breed innumerable maggots, with which

the earth, in spots, was alive. Especially was this the
case at all quarters where there were very sick men.
Then take into consideration the condition of the only
articles of clothing the sick were obliged to wear, and
had worn for months, without washing, and this, too,
in very warm weather, and one can gain some idea of
the misery endured by the thousands of sick men, and
the horrors of the prison in which they were confined.
Remember, also, that those who were in better health
had, in many instances, to sleep with those who were
sick, and eat their already filthy food drawn from the
rebels, amid all this additional contaminating dirt
and stench.

## "GRAYBACKS."

BUT this does not end the catalogue of miseries of
the sick prisoners. The inner portions of their
wretched clothing were alive with body-lice. Every-
body was beset with vermin of this kind, but those who
were in comparative health had not one where the sick
had a hundred. The reason why the garments of the
sick were so much more infested than those of others
was because those in better health could remove their
own garments and pick off these vermin, as the most
of them did everyday, while the invalids were unable
to do so. No doubt the question has arisen in the
minds of many readers, why did not the well ones look
after the clothing of the sick? In most cases they did
so, to the extent of their strength and ability.
Remember, I am describing the condition of the very
sick and debilitated patients. Remember, also, there
were very few really healthy ones in the prison, as
compared with the aggregate number of the prisoners.

Those who were quite strong were generally fresh arrivals from battlefields, and they, of course, kept together to preserve their health, and for other reasons.

In many of those quarters in which were the very sick and weak ones, there might not be a well man among the four or five who messed together. Most of them would be able, by exerting themselves, to pick the vermin from their own clothing, carry water, and draw and cook their rations; and, besides, to draw and prepare the rations of their sick, and supply them with water, was all the most of them were able to do.

### THE WAY OF THE WORLD.

If in your sympathy for the sick and very destitute of those whom I have been describing, the question presents itself, Why did not the well ones and new-comers, who were better able, separate themselves and each take a destitute and suffering comrade as a mess-mate and take care of him? Tell me why any rich man, in the United States, or elsewhere, does not invite a very shabby and destitute man to become his partner, instead of a man of equal wealth and standing, and the question is answered. Again, answer the question, Why do not the rich and comfortable ones in our cities take the worthy poor and destitute ones among them into their dwellings and take care of them? and the question is answered. Even professors of religion do not feel this to be their duty, except in a very few instances. They feel that their obligation is fully performed if they carry to them, occasionally, some little luxury or comfort. This was precisely the spirit and practice of the prisoners. If they were passing one of those destitute invalids and he wanted water, they would go with cup or canteen and get it for him, and do other acts of a similar nature.

If the rich of our cities can be excused for not taking the worthy poor into their dwellings, but prefer to bestow their care upon those who have plenty and to spare, surely those prisoners who were themselves destitute, having naught except a little strength, and being obliged at all times to do all they could to preserve their own lives, ought not to be criticized too sharply. It was not a struggle with us for wealth or honor, but for life.

### DEPRIVATIONS OF THE SICK.

Then, in addition to all this misery, many of the sick were in such a condition that they could not eat the miserable food in sufficient quantities to keep them long alive. I believe I have before stated that the thousands (for they numbered thousands) of sick ones inside the stockade did not receive any diet different from that drawn by others, whatever might be the stage of their diseases. Many had sore mouths, caused (as we supposed) by scurvy, with their gums eaten off and their teeth loosened, until it pained them to eat the dry cornbread that seemed to them more like sand in their mouths than food. Then there were many others who suffered from a disordered condition of the stomach, and from loss of appetite, to a degree that their food became repulsive to them.

### THE SCURVY.

All the prisoners had this disease, which we were informed was scurvy, to a greater or less degree, after they had been in prison a few weeks. It is not only exhibited in the mouth, but will increase, if the causes are not removed, until it extends throughout the whole system. A great many had it so severely that their limbs generally, from the knee down and including the feet, were swollen and inflamed, the skin cracked open, and that other terrible disease, gangrene (a slow type of mortification), would set in; then nothing but amputation of the affected part would save the patient's life.

With many the mortified flesh sloughed off, and left the naked bones of parts of the feet and ankles exposed to view. A large number of these sufferers would not request amputation, and many had no opportunity to do so; so they died from the effects of this disease, or from others in connection with it.

Those who were captured alone, having no blankets, or cooking intensils, or anything that possessed value in the prison, or if they had no intimate friends, did very well as long as they retained their health, and the cool weather kept off; but after that their condition became bad; then falling sick, and not receiving proper care, they usually perished in a short time.

As I close this chapter, the reader will remember that I have not been describing the inmates of a hospital, but sick men who were held as prisoners of war by a party (or class) of men who claimed a degree of civilization high enough then, and do yet, to govern this advanced nation. It was for this they rebelled. They not only held us as prisoners of war, but put us in a miserable pen, without shelter or medical treatment, and locked the gate and left us to die, coming in just often enough, and doing just enough, to ward off retaliation and foreign interference.

# CHAPTER VII.

Mortality Statistics—Modes of Burial—The Dead-Line—A Man Shot.

IT was impossible for so many men, crowded into so small a space, with such privations; with little opportunity for helping themselves; with the constantly increasing accumulation of filth during a hot, dry season; in a climate to which they were not accustomed, and subjected to the unnatural and filthy prison diet, to prevent the frequent occurrence of deaths.

## THE NUMBER OF THE SICK.

I am not prepared at present to state the daily or monthly average of mortality among us. Neither do I know how many died in the hospital; but the number must have been great, when it is considered that none but the very worst cases out of the numerous sick ones I have described were admitted to its shelter. But I occasionally went to the gate where they were carried and laid upon the ground, and counted them. Forty-five was the least number that I saw there in any one day, if my memory is correct, and I heard others declare that the number ran as high as seventy-five.

## DISPOSITION OF THE DEAD.

The custom was, when a prisoner died, if any one knew his name, company, regiment, etc., to write it on a piece of paper and fasten it on his shirt-bosom, thinking that the rebels would record it. We were informed that they did so. Each corpse was then carried up to the gate, where they were laid in rows. A vehicle, known as the "dead wagon," was subsequently driven up to the outside of the gate, the dead were loaded in, and then they were hauled off to the burying-ground. I was never at the burial place, but I was informed by our own men who did the burying—going out on that duty on parole, and drawing double rations for their services—that they dug long trenches, wide enough to lay the dead in cross-wise. There they were deposited side by side, without coffin or box, and buried. I know nothing of the record, if one was kept, or of the marks placed at the head of each corpse. I have understood that something of the kind was customarily done in that direction.

### THE DEAD-LINE.

BESIDES those who died with disease, others were shot by the guards for crossing the dead-line. Some, either partially or wholly, lost their reason, wandered over the fatal boundary, and were shot. Others, it is supposed, became discouraged; others despaired of ever getting out; and both of this class preferred to die rather than to continue to suffer as they did. These stepped over the dead-line and were killed.

Others were killed for lighter offenses. The plank that was used for a bridge in crossing the creek lay close by the dead-line pole. All the prisoners were permitted to cross it. One morning I had just passed over it when I heard the report of a gun in the hands of the guard who was stationed at that point. I turned to see the cause, and saw a man—a prisoner—flounder-

tions to what I was doing, but continued to watch for a victim, and every time a man was about to step on the crossing he would level his gun at him.

I had left the place, and in a few minutes I heard the report of the guard's gun; but I did not retrace my steps to see who had been shot. The reader may wonder why I did not return when the shot was fired, and why every other man in that vicinity did not hasten back to the scene of danger. There were two good reasons why we did not: First, the repetition of such events and the sight of dead men lying around, with many other circumstances quite as horrible, were too frequent to create excitement; and, secondly, the prisoners were not allowed to gather in crowds, except in special places and on certain occasions, such as in our market-place, when drawing our rations, at roll-call, etc.

Besides the guards, the rebels had batteries in position to sweep every part of the prison. The cannon were kept continually loaded with grape and canister-shot, and constantly manned. In addition to these safeguards, regiments of infantry were continuously stationed, as a reserve force, near the stockade.

# CHAPTER VIII.

IN addition to all their precautions to prevent the escape of prisoners, the roll was called every morning. The order of proceedings was as follows: The commissary of each company was obliged to have all his men in line at the moment the call was made. A rebel for every company was present to call the roll of each at precisely the same time, and each rebel knew how many men should be in the company assigned to him. The commissary had to account for all his men, as either in line, or sick, or dead, before they broke ranks. If he could not, it was taken for granted that the missing ones had escaped, and they were so reported. But, with all this vigilance and careful inspection, prisoners did sometimes escape.

### HOW THEY ESCAPED.

THEIR methods of escaping and eluding the watchfulness of their guards were numerous, odd, and frequently amusing. I will relate a few. One way was to tunnel under the stockade. A company would covenant among themselves, in secret, to dig a tunnel. Their manner of execution was to commence in some one's quarters near the dead-line, and work during the darkness of the night, to avoid detection by the guards. Some dug while others carried the dirt to the creek.

They did not dare to leave it in sight, lest it should betray them. The rebels were in the prison every morning, looking for signs of tunneling. The prisoners covered the entrances to their excavations with leaves, litter, or whatever they had under their blankets where they slept, and then arranged their quarters as usual through the day. Others commenced outside but close to some cave, or quarters.

It was tedious work, taking weeks to tunnel out. It was also discouraging, for many companies had been detected, or betrayed, by some one before they finished The rebels, anxious to find these tunnels, held out a strong inducement to such unprincipled men as we had among us, by granting a parole to the informer who exposed his comrades. Some were thus betrayed and defeated. Some escaped by their tunnels; but their trouble and danger were not over after they succeeded in getting outside, or their flight certain. The rebels always instituted a search outside of the stockade, every morning, for holes and other signs of an escapade. If any prisoners had flown at night, we could always know it by looking over the stockade.

### BLOODHOUNDS.

At such times we could see the rebel officers mounted on horses, with bloodhounds around them, and there were old men and boys, on old mules and horses, using sheepskins, old blankets and bags of hay for saddles, gathering for a grand hunt. They seemed to enjoy pursuing "Yanks" with those savage dogs more than frontiersmen ever delighted in wolf-hunting. When all were ready they took the hounds to the place of escape and put them on the track, and soon the chase

began, the men and boys pushing forward like a band
of wild Sioux Indians.

We could see, by the movements of the dogs, that
the prisoners generally proceeded to the creek, hoping,
by wading in its channel, to confuse the scent of the
dogs, which they knew would be put upon their track.
This did them but little service, however, for the company divided, with the dogs, and kept along both banks
till one set of the hounds struck the trail where the
fugitives left the creek.

Some escaped, but many were caught. If the latter
heard the baying of the dogs in time, climbed trees and
found mercy in the eyes of their pursuers, it was well;
but if not, they suffered the consequences of being over-
taken. Some bribed the guards with watches, or
money, or other valuables, which they had smuggled
into the prison.

### SHREWD TRICKS.

THE prisoners were in the habit of turning the large
bean-boxes down in the hinder ends of the wagons
that brought in the rations, and scraping off the beans
that stuck to the sides, while the front box was being
emptied. One man would get the others to turn down
the box over him while the rebel was busy with his
work. When the wagons were driven outside of the
stockade they were abandoned until the next day, and
under the cover of night the shrewd prisoner lifted up
the box, crawled out and fled unseen. There is no
telling how many escaped before this trick was exposed.

Another very daring experiment was tried by a
prisoner, who engaged his comrades to carry him and
lay him with the dead, arranging him on the top of the

corpses to be hauled out for burial. At that time the dead were not examined by the doctor, but were loaded by our own men, while the wagon was driven by a negro, unattended by a guard. The escaping prisoner watched for a favorable place to dismount, trusting that the negro (whose race were generally friendly to us when they could be) would comprehend the affair and say nothing. He therefore quietly slipped off from the wagon; but the superstitious driver thought the dead were coming to life, leaped from the wagon in fright, and ran off and reported the occurrence to the authorities.

### RELIGIOUS SERVICES.

There were but few religious services held in the prison, and but little regular praying that I heard. Everywhere men would express their feelings and anxiety in this direction with exclamations like the following: "The Lord have mercy on us!" "I wonder if the Lord will ever deliver us!" or, "God only knows what will become of us," and many other similar ejaculations.

Boston Corbett, the soldier who shot Booth, the assassin of President Lincoln, was with us and held religious services occasionally. I saw him eight years ago, and was for two days in a meeting with him. He was then living near Concordia, Cloud county, Kansas, on a claim. For some reason he did not care to be known, or gain notoriety by telling who he was, or talking about the event that immortalized his name on earth.

# CHAPTER IX.

Removal from Andersonville—Excitement—Arrival at Florence.

I HAVE arrived at the end of my narrative and description of Andersonville, and of what I saw and suffered there with others. Many things happened before I entered the prison and after I left it that I have not written, but of which I heard and believe to be true. If I had narrated what I heard from others, as several other writers have done, I could relate many incidents and particulars more shocking, if possible, than those I have recorded, but they would not be as trustworthy. With very few exceptions, I have written what I saw, and those exceptions are, that when I did not myself witness what occurred I have been careful to mention that fact.

### PROSPECTS OF FREEDOM.

It must have been about the last of October when Captain Wirz sent us word that we were all to be immediately exchanged, and that we would be taken to our lines as soon as transportation could be secured.

Many of the prisoners were almost wild with excitement—they were so confident of its truth. The sick and despondent revived and were cheered with the hope that they might get home to their friends at last. Others, who had previously been deceived by the rebels when they were transferred to Andersonville from Belle Island, Libby and other prisons, were doubtful. Still,

I believe, all thought the message might possibly be true.

There was one reason why it might be false. When the rebels wished to transfer prisoners from one stronghold to another, in part, they were accustomed to mislead as many as they could, by asserting that they were taking them out for an exchange. This was done to make the prisoners less anxious to escape during the transfer. This scheme was generally successful, for the most of the men were credulous, and did not try to elude the vigilance of their guards.

### LEAVING THE PRISON.

IMMEDIATELY after this intelligence reached us, the rebels made up freight trains of box-cars, taking out a load of us everyday. At first they called for us by companies, as we were organized; but those who firmly believed that an exchange was in progress became anxious, left their own companies, and flanked out with those who were first called. The rebels seemed to care nothing for this infraction of discipline; and the result was that in a day or two those who could crowd out ahead till a train was full went first. Of course, more than an average of the well and strongest prisoners were thus first transported. I went out, I think, the second day after the transfer began—not that I had much confidence in the story of an exchange, but I felt that we could not be sent to a worse place, and that it might be better. As many as could be were crowded into a box-car, with one guard stationed in the sliding-doorway, while many more were carried on top of the car.

Nothing worthy of note occurred during our trip to

Charleston, S. C., which was our destination, and where, the rebels said, arrangements had been made for our exchange.

### AT CHARLESTON.

ARRIVING at Charleston, we were corralled on a piece of ground in the rear of the city, where we were reasonably well-guarded; not to an extent, however, that would excite suspicion among those who still believed in a speedy exchange.

We remained here, I presume, ten days, waiting (the rebels said) for the officers to perfect arrangements for the exchange. From our quarters we could see the shells from the Union gunboats bursting in the city everyday. I must admit that the prospects for an exchange did look slightly favorable on coming to Charleston and during our encampment there.

### A SURPRISE.

THE question arose in my mind: "If they don't mean exchange, why did they bring us here?" I knew they could not hold us prisoners in an open field. But we did not understand everything. They were preparing a stockade, similar to that at Andersonville, at Florence, eighty miles from Charleston. One day we were ordered to "fall in—ranks," and marched to the railway station, where we were again loaded into box-cars, strongly guarded, and sent to Florence prison. There we were once more, turned into a stockade. How many doubtful prisoners escaped during this transfer we have no way of knowing, but no doubt many did.

# CHAPTER X.

In Prison Again—Cool Weather—A Three Days' Fast—Additional Suffering.

IN describing Florence prison much of the labor has been performed in the preceding sketches of Andersonville experiences. Many things were similar, and I shall avoid repetitions unless it shall be deemed necessary.

Florence stockade was patterned after that at Andersonville, but was much smaller. It is supposed that there were not, at any one time, more than 10,000 prisoners within it. The health and condition of the prisoners on entering Florence was better, on an average, than at Andersonville. This may be accounted for if we consider the manner in which we left Andersonville—the strongest crowding out first—and considering the fact, also, that the transfer to Florence was stopped about the time one-third of the prisoners had been let out. However, a great many feeble ones were also crowded out, in their anxiety for freedom, and landed in Florence.

### BEGINNING ANEW.

WHEN I arrived the prisoners were almost all there. I was unfortunate again in not getting through in time to secure any of the wood and brush that had been left inside after the stockade was built. The first prisoners in had gathered it and built them quite comfortable quarters, of various kinds, to winter in, and wood enough to last them quite a while. In fact, on my arrival, wood was so scarce that many had already commenced digging up the tree-stumps and roots for fuel.

I had become separated from my own company boys, and had fallen in with a sick man by the name of Cross, of Company A, my regiment, who had been able to get through to Florence. He had a blanket, a five-quart tin pail, a fry-pan, a spoon, cup, canteen, etc., but was almost unable to help himself. I gladly accepted the opportunity of drawing his rations, doing the cooking, and carrying the water, in exchange for the use of his outfit. I had a blanket, in addition to his, which placed us in pretty good condition, as compared with that of many others. But we had no shelter. We could not make a cave without some poles and sticks to hold up the dirt. The nights were getting cold, for South Carolina, and we preferred to have the blankets over us rather than make a tent out of them. We dug a hole in the ground, about two feet deep, and long and broad enough to lie down in, and covered ourselves with the blankets. This excavation served to shelter us from the wind.

### A SEVERE TRIAL.

DURING the period we slept in this hole came the severest struggle for life in my prison experiences. There came on a trying, cold, windy time, unusual in South Carolina, which lasted three days. We were unprepared, with our threadbare and ragged summer garments, for such a trial, having but little strength and vitality, and hungry and discouraged. But this was not the worst feature of our situation. The rebels

and wondering if they could possibly live through another such a dreadful night as that which was surely coming.

The second day and night passed about the same, but with increased suffering and more numerous deaths.

### RELIEF.

I DO not know whether the rebels found the tunnel, or not, but the third day of our fast they brought in rations. They did not issue any rations for the days when we had none, but for one day, and of about the quantity apportioned at Andersonville.

### MORTALITY.

I CANNOT tell you how many deaths occurred during those terrible three days, but they were many. Some may think three days not a long time to fast. Such treatment could be endured by a fleshy, well-clothed and well-fed person, in good health, and under more favorable circumstances, without danger; but take a half-starved, lean, weakly person, not half-clad, in the cold winds, without fire or food, and the contrast is so great that it can be comprehended by only a few individuals.

# CHAPTER XI.

I WAS in Florence prison at the time—the fall of
1864—when Lincoln was elected President for a
second term.

On election-day—whether by the request of the
rebels, or in accordance with the wishes of the leading
prisoners, I know not—arrangements were made to let
us vote in harmony with our political tendencies. Both
the rebels and the prisoners became interested in the
affair. A ballot-box was prepared, and the rebels
furnished black and white beans for ballots. The black
beans—representing the black abolitionists—were for
Lincoln, and the white ones for McClellan. We were
permitted to go up by companies and vote. I do not .
remember that there was any compulsion in the matter,
and I never learned what proportion of the prisoners
voted; but when the votes were counted, Lincoln had
five to McClellan's two. This was a great surprise to
the rebels, who hated Lincoln, and during the whole
period of our imprisonment they had not ceased their
endeavors to make us believe that he was to blame for
our not being exchanged—declaring that they were
ready to exchange at any time. They supposed that
the prisoners were prejudiced against Lincoln for this
reason; but the election proved to them that we had as
much sense as themselves, and more principle than they

had of deception. Their interest in the election, therefore, was in favor of McClellan.

### DEATH OF A COMRADE.

WITHIN a few days after our terrible fast, my
partner died, and I fell heir to his blanket, pail, fry-pan,
canteen and other things in his possession. I could not
prevent his death; but, as is frequently the case in life,
his taking-off placed me in a condition to improve my
situation. I had no cave, or shelter, but knew that with
my present outfit I could get into one that had not these
conveniences. However, I did not immediately take
advantage of the opportunity, but took in a destitute
cousin, Mr. Weidman, who had gone blind since his
imprisonment. I took care of him until he went out
on a special exchange of sick, in December. He died
at Annapolis, Md., on the road home, in one of the
hospitals. Before he died he got the nurse to write to
my wife, telling her that I was still alive, where I was,
and my condition.

### CHANGES.

AFTER the exchange of my cousin, I made arrangements with another party for new quarters. I was
acquainted with a mess of three, who had a very good
cave, large enough for them to sit in, side by side, and
to lie down in, but not high enough to stand up in, but
to kneel in. One of them was very sick. The other
two were very anxious that I should come in with them
as soon as he died. I consented to do so.

During the interval I joined a man in a small cave,
which was so low that we could hardly sit upright in
it, and the entrance so small that we had to crawl in and

out. I was with him only a few days before he was taken ill, and became insane. In this condition he was cross, ungovernable and somewhat dangerous, so that in caring for him I had my hands full, until he again became rational. His insanity did not last long, and he soon began to improve.

A few days later one of the three men with whom I had arranged to join came and told me that their sick partner was dead; whereupon I immediately gathered up my things and removed to their quarters.

Upon arriving there I found that they had just laid the dead man outside of the cave, and he was lying near the entrance when I approached it. He had probably been dead half-an-hour, and had been removed about five minutes when I put my things in his place.

We lived very agreeably together during our stay in Florence.

### OUR DIET, AGAIN.

AFTER entering this prison we found the provisions were inferior, in quantity, to the rations at Andersonville, and composed, almost exclusively, of one article—corn-meal. They gave us a pint a day of it, of about the same quality as that at Andersonville, unbolted. Some made it into cakes as best they could, some into mush; others preferred it in gruel. I saw one man eating his raw meal mixed up with water—the only case of the kind that I witnessed, but I heard of others who did so. Many ate it at one meal, and waited for more than twenty-four hours, or until ration-time came around again. After getting into my last quarters, we three agreed to make two meals of our rations, to make it into gruel, and to cook it all in my five-quart tin pail.

We did not make it into gruel because we liked it best in that form, but for the greater length of time it required to eat it. Numbers of others ate it in this manner for the same reason. With many this food agreed, except that it gradually developed the scurvy in their systems. It was so with me. During my prison-life—except when I had a bilious attack that lasted three days, and another day's sickness that I may hereafter mention— I was so hungry, even after I had eaten my allowance, that I used frequently to say, "If I live to get out of here, I will never complain as long as I can get all the corn-bread I want."

### FUEL.

We had a small chimney at the end of our cave, made of mud and clay, with the hands. Chimneys made in this manner were quite common. We had a small fire-place, a foot wide, at the base. In this we hung our tin pail, a few inches above the ground. On account of the scarcity of wood, we cut it up into splinters, averaging a quarter-inch in thickness, and six inches in length. We would keep five or six of these ablaze, under the center of the pail, in such a manner that none of the heat should be lost. In this way we could make five quarts of gruel with a bunch of splinters as large as one's arm. I have been particular in giving these details, to show how the prisoners had to economize.

### HOW WE ATE.

After my messmates and myself had cooked our gruel, we would sit around the pail and dip into it regularly, by turns, till it was gone. One of our mess was quite old, and he frequently used to say, when the gruel became low in the pail, "I hate to see the bottom!"

Things went on in this way for quite awhile; when, one day, the others told me, in as kindly a manner as they could, that my spoon was larger than theirs, and they hardly thought they could stand it. They seemed to be afraid that I would be offended and leave them. But I told them that I thought so myself; and after that I ate my ration alone. I had discovered the fact of which they complained some time before, but quieted my conscience by the thought that I was furnishing the largest share of the outfit of the mess, and by trying to believe that this circumstance made the matter all right. But this excuse will not bear the test of honesty, let alone religion.

In addition to the pint of meal issued daily to a prisoner, the rebels, once or twice a week, gave each of us a tablespoonful of beans, measured to us with a spoon. Few had wood to cook them, and many ate them raw, as I did.

### WOOD, AGAIN.

The rebels issued wood, but not in quantities sufficient to keep up fire in cold or chilly weather; after it had been divided among us it amounted to one stick to each prisoner—about the size of a man's arm—per day.

### MORE MORTALITY.

Sickness and death increased from the time we entered this prison until we went out. This is proven by the fact that 3,000 sick men, out of 10,000 prisoners, were taken from it on a special exchange, in December. Many sick ones remained after this number had been taken. Numbers of destitute ones died of colds, many of chronic disease of the bowels, and others gradually starved to death.

The question may be asked, how could a part of the prisoners live so long on the apportioned quantity of provisions, and of such quality, while others died so soon? I answer by another question: Why some cattle, in many countries, when feed is scarce, turned out to browse through the winter, will starve while others thrive? This answer will serve for both inquiries. It will be borne in mind that the food did not agree with many, and became repulsive to them at sight, while with others it was nourishing, and they never lost their relish for it.

### OUR DREAMS.

Those who retained a good appetite and were desperately hungry all the time would tell each other what they should consider palatable food. One would say that if he had a certain dish, such as his mother or his wife used to make, it certainly would be the best on earth; and all would agree with him, until some one else would suggest another dish, describing it, and then they would all change their decision and give it the preference. Whatever we could get our minds fixed upon last was deemed the best. Our stomachs were ready for anything. A starving man has but little choice. It is nourishment that he craves. We would think and talk of these things during the day, and dream about them at night. In these visions we would be at home and sitting down at a well-filled table, waiting for the cooks to arrange the preliminaries before we could commence to eat. I have dreamed that if they knew how hungry I was they would not keep me waiting so long. But when I awoke—it was all a dream, with no prospect of going home.

# CHAPTER XII.

IT would be an impossibility to collect as many men in one institution as we had in Florence prison, or that at Andersonville, regardless of moral character, without including among them thieves and robbers. Where there is no law, and no penalty to fear, if men are naturally inclined to do wrong, they will show out their propensities under such circumstances as those in which we were placed. Owing to the presence of such characters among us, we were compelled to organize a police force before we left Andersonville, and this was done with the sanction of the rebel authorities. It will be remembered that the managers of the prison did not endeavor to keep us orderly among ourselves; they were principally interested in preventing our escape. The police system was, at first, a great blessing, but soon after we entered the stockade at Florence it became more of a curse than a blessing.

There were two large, stout, hearty men, whom we called Pete and Stanton, both prisoners, but rebels at heart. They catered to all the rebels' wishes, and were tools in their hands. They were just such men as the rebels could use to good advantage in many ways. They manifested no desire to escape, for the rebels gave them about all the privileges they wanted, and fed them well. They were friends to our enemies, and traitors to the prisoners, and, through their influence with the rebels, succeeded in forcing themselves, arbitrarily, upon us as chiefs of police. In this position they appointed subordinates, of their own choosing, who would do their bidding in everything, in order to retain their offices. It was a desirable situation, for all police received double rations. I think that in Florence we had as truly a despotic government among ourselves as there is on earth. The tyrants, Stanton and Pete, made all the laws, without even the voice of the other police. They gave orders to their corps of police, and these were carried out to the letter.

### THE WHIPPING-POST.

THEY established a whipping-post, and the lash was used for all offenses. It was a hundred lashes on the bare back for stealing. If a man was caught selling his rations, he was whipped. If he failed to reach the private quarters he received the same punishment, and a similar one for several other infractions of their laws; but these will serve as specimens of their arbitrary rule, and they seemed anxious to find occasion for inflicting this penalty. But little evidence of the guilt of parties was required.

The instrument of torture was made of a heavy strap of leather, about eighteen inches long, split into four equal parts, and fastened to a suitable stock or handle. Twenty-five strokes with this were counted one hundred lashes.

I have seen Stanton make a victim bare his back from the shoulders to the hips, and order him to kneel. Then Stanton, in a sitting posture, would take the victim's head between his knees, while another policeman, who relished the job, gave the unfortunate man twenty-five blows with this terrible instrument of torture. I have seen the muscles in the victim's back crawl up into knots while undergoing such a flagellation.

### NEW SPECULATIONS.

BEFORE the rule of the police prohibiting the sale of their rations by the prisoners was enforced, many who had no conveniences for cooking would sell their raw provisions and purchase cooked ones. Those who had cooking utensils baked cakes and took them to the market-place and sold them to those who were in the habit of selling their raw rations. Then they would buy meal and bake more, taking care to make a good profit in the operation. Of those who sold prepared food, many took their money and bought tobacco. This they cut up into "chews" as large as they thought they could afford, after making a careful calculation; then go through the prison crying, "Who will have a chew of tobacco for a spoonful of meal?" and so many were ready to trade that, in some cases, a permanent and extensive business was established. The meal thus obtained would be cooked and exchanged for more tobacco, and thus the supply was constantly kept up.

Another enterprise was quite extensively carried on. Many of the prisoners who were in poor health did not feel like procuring water for themselves, especially in bad weather. Some of the more rugged ones took advantage of this opportunity, and would go about the prison crying, "Who will have a pail of water for a spoonful of meal?"

# CHAPTER XIII.

Leaving the Prison—Released from Durance—Home Again.

ABOUT February 15 we received two days' rations with an order to be ready to leave the prison. The cause of this movement was Sherman's successful march to the sea, and his capture of Savannah and Charleston. His army was then only eighty miles from us, and the rebels knew that some of his forces would reach Florence, within a few days, and release us.

To prevent this the rebels hurried us out, intending to transfer us to Salisbury, N. C., for safe keeping; but they soon found themselves circumscribed—their rope was getting short. So they once more loaded us, like stock, into box-cars, packing as many of us as could be crowded into each and live, and started with us for the determined destination, via Wilmington and Goldsborough, N. C. By the time we reached the latter place the rebels learned that part of Sherman's army had cut them off by getting between them and Salisbury, at a point on the railroad. Thus headed off in this direction, they had but one more course that they could take, and that was toward Richmond, Va. But Grant, they learned, had succeeded in cutting the only line of railroad leading to that place. It was, therefore, a matter of very brief time before we would be taken from them without an exchange. They kept us at Goldsborough a few days, while they were making arrangements to exchange us or surrender us to our government at Wilmington.

### ON THE MOVE.

To this end they sent us back to that place; but before our arrival there, a part of Sherman's army had attacked the city, and the general in charge would not consent to a truce long enough to arrange to receive us and make the exchange. The reason of this was, we were informed, that the loss of time would give the rebels an opportunity to remove their supplies out of the city.

We were, therefore, kept in the background for a short season, while the Union attack on Wilmington was in progress; and on the day the city was captured we were again loaded into cars and sent back to Goldsborough.

While at Wilmington, the last time, I had the privilege of walking around among the sick, who had been brought out of Florence last. They had been taken out of the cars, and were lying on the ground by the side of the railroad track. There must have been at least a thousand of them; many of them very sick, some dying, and others had been released by death. As I passed along among them, I came to a man with whom I had formed an early acquaintance in Andersonville. His name was Hadden, and we had become intimates from the fact that his wife's brother was a member of my company. I saw and talked with him every few days. He was very destitute, but braced up, and did not succumb to his circumstances. When I left Florence he was considerably reduced, but moving about; when I found him at Wilmington he was dead.

I mention this particular case, for the reason that I had learned his wife's name and address; and after I arrived at home I wrote to her, told her the facts, and was an important witness in securing a pension for her. Otherwise it would have been difficult for her to obtain it.

In the same manner I aided Mrs. Cross to procure a pension. Cross, it will be remembered (see Chapters X. and XI.), was the man to whose effects I fell heir at Florence. His home was at Effingham, Ill. Hadden lived in New Jersey.

### LIVING TOO HIGH.

I ALLUDED, in a previous chapter, to a day's sickness I experienced, and will now enter more fully into the particulars of that event, although it comes into my narrative rather late.

After drawing our rations at Florence, on the day of leaving there, I made and ate a larger mess than usual of mush and beans, cooked together. The beans had been issued as part of the rations for that special occasion, and by the time I entered the car I was terribly sick. I was in such a condition, under the circumstances, that I almost despaired of recovery, thinking that there was no relief for me, and gave away the rations that I had drawn and cooked for the trip; yet I grew better the same day and soon became very hungry; but by my foolish act in giving away my provisions, I had to suffer the consequences until we reached Goldsborough.

Some may wonder why we did not try to escape while we were being moved about. No doubt many did, while others were not able to do so. Most of us knew, before our first return to Wilmington, that everything denoted a parole, or exchange. The majority knew that it would be only a delay of a few days until we should be inside the Union lines. The rebels could not keep the facts in regard to the operations and success of our army from us any longer, nor did they try to do so.

We did not remain at Goldsborough more than two or three days before we were paroled and loaded upon flat-cars and in box-cars and started again to Wilmington. I was sitting on the edge of a flat-car, and as we came to a curve in the road, just after leaving Goldsborough, I looked forward and saw a white flag on the engine. This was something I had never before seen, but I knew it was a flag of truce. This sight settled all doubts.

### LIBERTY.

I WILL not attempt to describe my feelings in full; but I thought, after all my doubts and anxieties about my destiny, during the past months of misery and suffering, in a few hours I shall once more see the Stars and Stripes, and be again a free man. Then I thought that I should soon see home and hear of friends from whom I had not received any intelligence for seven months. I did not know that my wife was aware that I still lived. I supposed she was with my other friends, and deemed me dead. I had been captured all alone, away from my company and regiment, and I could not conceive how they would know what became of me in that terrible day of slaughter—July 22, 1864.

We arrived at the Union line, near Wilmington, on the morning of February 28, 1865. The line was a wagon-road, on one side of which floated the Union flag, with our officers and soldiers in full uniform and armed; on the other were the rebel flag and armed officers and soldiers of the "Confederacy;" on one side was rebeldom, and on the other, as the prisoners expressed it, was "God's country."

The engine was run up to the road, and we immediately debarked from the cars, marching single-file across the highway, between the open ranks of a detachment of soldiers, an officer from both armies counting us as we passed through.

Thank the good Lord! we were out of the hands of tyrants and once more free!

### GOING HOME.

WE remained in Wilmington two or three days; then went on board a vessel, sailed along the coast and up the bay to Annapolis, Md. Here we each exchanged, with the government, our rags for a suit of new clothes, and, soon after, were on our way, by rail, to St. Louis, Mo. Upon our arrival there we were granted furloughs, and I went home to Newtown, Livingston County, Ill.

The first person I met after reaching home was my wife. She saw me coming and met me. She was not keeping house, but staying with one of my uncles. She was expecting me, for I had written to her that I was released and on the way home.

I was discharged from the army at Springfield, Ill., June 3, 1865, having served three years, ten months and one day. Seven months and five days I had been a prisoner of war.

### THE FORTUNES OF WAR.

ONE fact I have hitherto neglected to mention. I had but ten days to serve, at the time of my capture, my term of enlistment being thus near its close. Within a fortnight I should probably have been out of the army and on my way home.

BEFORE closing my narrative, I will address a few words to prisoners who were with me in Andersonville and Florence. No doubt I have written many things that you did not see, although we were in the same prison. If you were to write a book you would no doubt record many facts that I did not ascertain. None of us saw one-half, or one-tenth—I do not know but I would be safe in saying one-hundredth—of the suffering endured in those prisons. I have related a few things that I saw and know.

Another thought: It may be that you did not make as many removals as I with others did before we were released. We began to scatter after the first break at Andersonville. I know that every time we moved our numbers grew less until we were released. I have told the particulars of the time, place and manner of release of those with whom I was at the time. You may have been passed through the lines at a different place and date.

Hoping that these suggestions may answer some questions that might arise, I will close.

THE END.

# FINALE.

My Second Imprisonment, Twenty-two Years after the Anderson-ville Confinement.--Written in the Winter.

We in our human coop remain
From morn till eve without much change.
We through our frosty window peer
In search of something new to cheer.

We are not prisoners for crime,—
Locked up by law to pay a fine,
For violating laws of State,—
Laws that the people did create.

But prisoners for another cause,
For violating nature's laws,—
Although compelled to many times,
Which leaves our conscience free from crime.

Disease and sickness are the chain
That fastened on our mortal frame;
That binds us fast and makes us slaves
For violating wisdom's ways.

And nature's weather is the guard—
Keeps us in bounds of cell and yard,
And circumstances are the key
That locks our door—we cannot flee.

A prisoner: yet not in despair;
Our hopes are bright, our prospects fair.
Our Judge is merciful and kind;
He's pardoned millions of mankind
For moral crimes, of every grade.
He healed the sick, gave sight to blind;
Why should we not his mercy find?

## *Finale.*

I know he will my health restore—
He may do that, he may do more:
Transport me to that world unseen,
Where everything is always green.

In that bright clime there is no grief,
There nothing can disturb our peace;
No blasted hopes in middle life;
Once there, we end this mortal strife.

www.ingramcontent.com/pod-product-compliance
Lightning Source LLC
Chambersburg PA
CBHW022152090426
42742CB00010B/1478